"ellipsis..."

ENDA O'DONOGHUE
Paintings 2007-2005

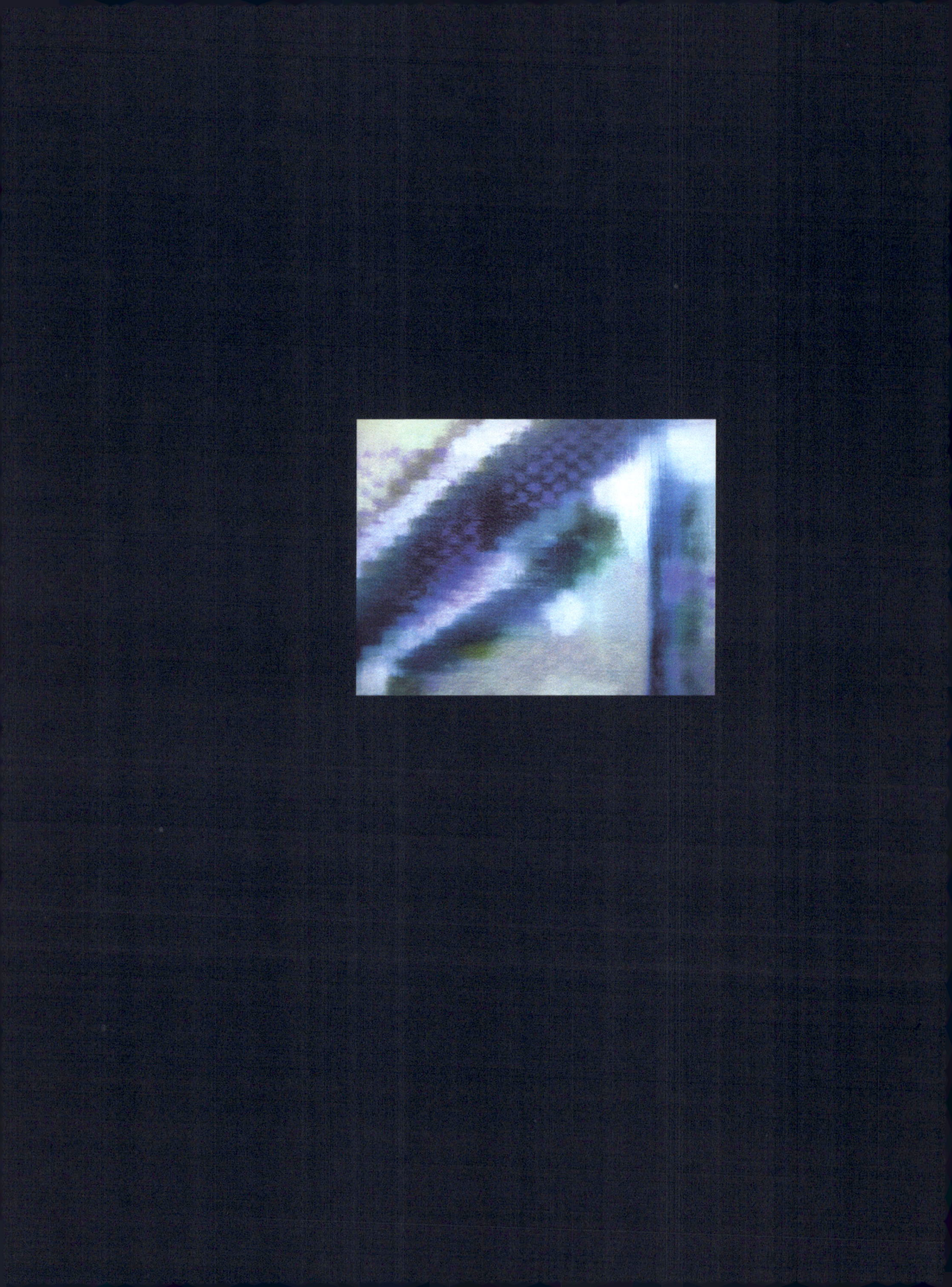

"ellipsis…"

Enda O'Donoghue has spoken of the 'in-between' spaces that inhabit his paintings; his interest in the physical characteristics of such places as airports, train stations, waiting rooms, shopping queues links to a theme familiar in European culture: our folk-tales and images are saturated with those spaces that straddle pastoral and urban, reason and emotion, fact and fiction, past and present.

The interstices of cultural life present particular challenges to the artist in that they are often among the most mundane images of contemporary existence. '…man exists, turns up, appears on the scene, and only afterwards, defines himself', comments Sartre. Waiting, 'between two worlds', is a time when we meet ourselves; there is nothing to do, no distraction, just the human and his or her existence. We look for a paper, a chat, a sleep, an argument, (as Beckett knew so well), to fill that space.

Enda O'Donoghue's artistic practice flows through varied media and thematic interests but this concern with the situatedness of the human condition is a consistent thread. His creative projects have involved the intersections of sound and image, and of video, photography, interactive media and painting; this has generated an exciting body of work which has been enriched by an appreciation of the applications of technology. The ancient art and craft of painting is defamiliarised by the infusion of the new; the computer and the brush or stencil are joined in a common cause, an interrogation of the shifts and turns of everyday experience.

The common nature of this experience is embodied in the problem of ownership that these images foreground. In a sense they are communal property but also the work of a single individual. They exist in multiple form but they can also be termed 'original'.

Music sampling has faced similar issues and the pains that O'Donoghue takes to rework these images evidences his understanding and interest in such issues. 'Copy' as in copyright takes on a new definition in an era of cloning, cyberspace and transplants. These paintings began their life as digital photographs on the internet. An artistic energy and sensitive vision has excavated and re-contextualised them. O'Donoghue has referred to this shift from digital image to painting as an act of translation. He traces ownership of the images, requests permission for their use and begins the process of shifting the image to the medium of a painting, through making a slide and sketching the photograph on canvas. The making of the painting is a dense, highly skilled and lengthy act: as 'translator' he seeks to maintain features of the original works which are often chosen because they offer a rawness of experience. The low resolution, pixelation, digital noise and glitches are the areas that interest the artist and he seeks to maintain these qualities in the finished work. *First Day New Job* and *Waiting to be called* bring out the poignancy of this deliberate downplaying of the surface of the image; the images possess a melancholy rootlessness matching their subject matter. Edward Said speaks of waiting as '...unending expectation, about the moment that comes before something which itself never comes, but which in the process reduces everyone to a frozen state of clown-like, pathetic banality in which only limited motion is possible in virtually the same places'. In the foreground of *Registration*, a man in profile stares blankly into space; the room we are shown is crowded with people who are literally, by being seen from the back, faceless. In other paintings territorial imperatives are reduced to the possession of a seat in a commuter train or a favoured place in a waiting room, temporary nomadic jostlings – these images disturb through their terrifying ordinariness.

Yet the work we see also celebrates. *Pray*, for instance, emphasises the gestural chant and dance that lies between physical and metaphysical, a defining archetype of our search for meaning in an increasingly homogenised world. Such images began in the mind's eye of untrained photographers using the mobile phone or digital camera, devices that put a power into the hands of the amateur, and these photos demonstrate the curious nature of our species. Someone found this or that moment worthy of recording and one aspect of the work is the quirky selectiveness that is highlighted by those choices. What O'Donoghue has done is to convert this 'pathetic banality' into the stuff of art while respecting the integrity of the muffled and occluded images that he has found. The internet is an instrument of democracy as well as of surveillance and this exhibition offers a template for the commonality of our concerns. Shaping and magnifying the images, applying stencil to analogise the low resolution of the photos, stamping and moving paint around to highlight the suggestive imperfections of the original indicates O'Donoghue's concern with this dimension of the work.

The translation we are offered is a collaborative event, a staging – the image-maker, the artist and the audience meet through moments that evoke the transient qualities of those nomadic spaces where the in-between happens, threaded as it is with the lonely relationships mandated by the queue, the bureaucracy, the working life.

Brian Coates

Dr Brian Coates is Director of Cultural Studies at the Bhasha Research and Publication Centre, Baroda, Gujarat, India and Research Fellow at the Interaction Design Centre, University of Limerick, Ireland.

»ellipse...«

Enda O'Donoghue hat einmal von den Räumen des »Dazwischen« gesprochen, die auf seinen Gemälden zu sehen sind;
sein Interesse an den physischen Charakteristika solcher Orte
wie Flughäfen, Bahnhöfen, Warteräumen, Warteschlangen beim
Einkaufen ist mit einem vertrauten Thema europäischer Kultur
verbunden: unsere Folktales und Vorstellungswelten sind durch-
setzt mit solchen Räumen, die das Ländliche und Urbane, Ver-
nunft und Gefühl, Fakt und Fiktion, Vergangenheit und Gegen-
wart überspannen.

Die Zwischenräume des kulturellen Lebens stellen eine beson-
dere Herausforderung für den Künstler dar, da sie oft zu den
alltäglichsten Bildern der zeitgenössischen Existenz gehören.
»... der Mensch existiert, erscheint auf der Bühne, und erst hin-
terher definiert er sich«, kommentiert Sartre. Warten, »zwischen
zwei Welten«, ist eine Zeit, in der wir uns erfahren; es gibt nichts
zu tun, keine Ablenkung, nur den Menschen und seine oder ihre
Existenz. Wir warten auf die Zeitung, auf einen Plausch, auf den
Schlaf, auf einen Wortwechsel (wie Beckett so genau wusste),
um diese Lücke zu füllen.

Enda O'Donoghues künstlerische Praxis durchfließt verschie-
dene Medien und thematische Interessen, wobei die Beschäfti-
gung mit dem Stellenwert der Conditio humana den roten Faden
bildet. Zu seinen kreativen Projekten gehörten das Zusammen-
spiel von Sound und Bild, und von Video, Fotografie, interaktiven
Medien und Malerei. So ist ein aufregendes Werk entstanden,
bereichert noch durch die vom Künstler geschätzte Technologie-
anwendung. Das alte Handwerk Malerei wird durch die Infusion
des Neuen dem Vertrauten entzogen; der Computer und der Pin-
sel oder die Schablone dienen einer gemeinsamen Sache, der
Untersuchung der Veränderungen der Alltagserfahrung.

Das Gemeinsame dieser Erfahrung liegt im Problem der Eigen-
tümerschaft, das diese Bilder aufwerfen. In gewisser Weise sind
sie gemeinschaftliches Eigentum, doch auch das Werk eines

einzigen Individuums. Sie existieren in multipler Form, können jedoch auch als ›Original‹ bezeichnet werden. Das Sampling von Musik hat ähnliche Fragen aufgeworfen, und die Anstrengungen, die O'Donoghue unternimmt, um diese Bilder zu bearbeiten, zeugen von seinem Verständnis solcher Probleme und von seinem Interesse daran. ›Copy‹, wie in Copyright, verlangt im Zeitalter des Klonens, des Cyberspace und der Transplantationen nach einer neuen Definition. Diese Gemälde begannen ihr Leben als Digitalfotos im Internet. Mit künstlerischer Energie und einer ausgeprägten Vorstellungskraft wurden sie ausgegraben und rekontextualisiert. O'Donoghue hat diesen Übergang vom Digitalbild zum Gemälde als Akt der Übersetzung bezeichnet. Er spürt der Urheberschaft der Bilder nach, bittet um Genehmigung, sie verwenden zu dürfen, und macht sich daran, das Bild ins Medium der Malerei zu übertragen, indem er ein Dia schießt und das Foto auf der Leinwand skizziert. Das Malen ist ein aufwändiger, hohe Fertigkeiten erfordernder, langer Akt: als ›Übersetzer‹ versucht er, Merkmale der Originale zu erhalten, deren Auswahl oft deswegen erfolgt, weil sie eine Rohheit der Erfahrung bieten. Die geringe Auflösung, die Pixelung, das Bildrauschen und digitale Störungen interessieren den Künstler, der versucht, seinem Endprodukt diese Eigenschaften einzuschreiben. Bei ›First Day New Job‹ und ›Waiting to be called‹ zeigt sich die absichtliche Vernachlässigung der Bildoberfläche deutlich; den Bildern ist ein melancholisches Entwurzeltsein eigen, das ihrem Thema entspricht. Edward Said spricht vom Warten als »... unaufhörlicher Erwartung, wegen des Moments, der vor etwas kommt, das selbst nie kommt, das jedoch im Prozess jeden in einen clown-ähnlichen Zustand pathetischer Banalität erstarren lässt, in dem Bewegung an den praktisch selben Orten nur begrenzt möglich ist.« Im Vordergrund von ›Registration‹ starrt ein im Profil zu sehender Mann ausdruckslos in den Raum; dieser ist voll von Leuten, die tatsächlich gesichtslos sind, weil sie von hinten betrachtet werden müssen. Auf anderen Gemälden ist das Räumliche auf die Verfügung über einen Sitzplatz in einem Nahverkehrszug oder einen bevorzugten Platz in einem Warteraum reduziert, temporäres nomadisches Gedrängel – das erschreckend Alltägliche dieser Bilder verstört.

Doch das Werk, das wir sehen, zelebriert auch. ›Pray‹, zum Beispiel, hebt den gestischen Gesang und Tanz hervor, der zwischen dem Physischen und Metaphysischen liegt, ein entscheidender Archetypus unserer Sinnsuche in einer zunehmend homogenisierten Welt. Die Bilder nahmen ihren Anfang im Geiste von Hobbyfotografen, die ihr Mobiltelefon oder ihre Digitalkamera benutzten, Gerätschaften, die Amateuren Macht in die Hand geben. Die Fotos verweisen auf die Neugier unserer Spezies. Irgendwer fand, dass dieser oder jener Augenblick festgehalten werden müsse, wobei die seltsame Wahl ein hervorstechender Aspekt des Ganzen ist. O'Donoghue verwandelt diese »pathetische Banalität« in Kunst, wobei er die Integrität der von ihm gefundenen undeutlichen oder der Okklusion unterliegenden Bilder respektiert. Das Internet ist ein Instrument der Demokratie wie der Überwachung, und diese Ausstellung bietet eine Plattform für unsere gemeinsame Besorgnis. Die Bearbeitung und Vergrößerung der Bilder, die Verwendung von Schablonen zur Analogisierung der niedrigen Auflösung der Bilder, das Herauslösen und Bewegen der Farbe, um die suggestiven Mangelhaftigkeiten des Originals zu betonen, verweisen darauf, wie wichtig O'Donoghue diese Dimension der Arbeit ist.

Die Übersetzung, die uns angeboten wird, ist ein gemeinschaftliches Ereignis, eine Inszenierung – der Bildmacher, der Künstler und das Publikum begegnen sich durch Momente, welche die flüchtigen Eigenschaften dieser nomadischen Räume evozieren, in denen sich das Dazwischen ereignet. Dieses ist verknüpft mit den einsamen Beziehungen, die dem Mandat der Warteschlange, der Bürokratie und dem Arbeitsleben unterstellt sind.

Brian Coates

Dr. Brian Coates leitet die Abteilung Kulturwissenschaften am Research and Publication Centre, Baroda, Gujarat, Indien und ist Gastwissenschaftler am Interaction Design Centre, University of Limerick, Irland.

Aus dem Englischen übersetzt von Jürgen Schneider.

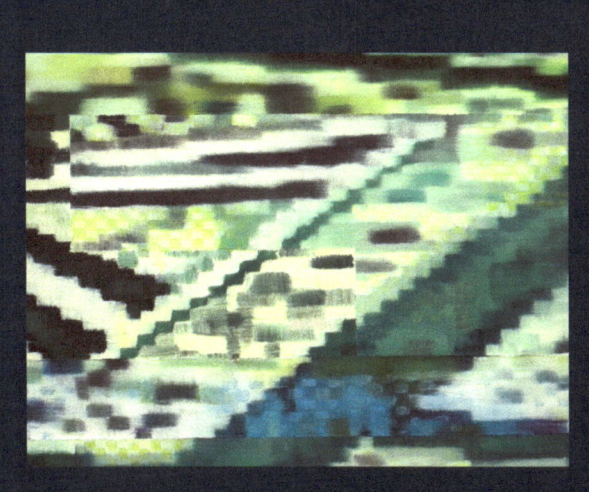

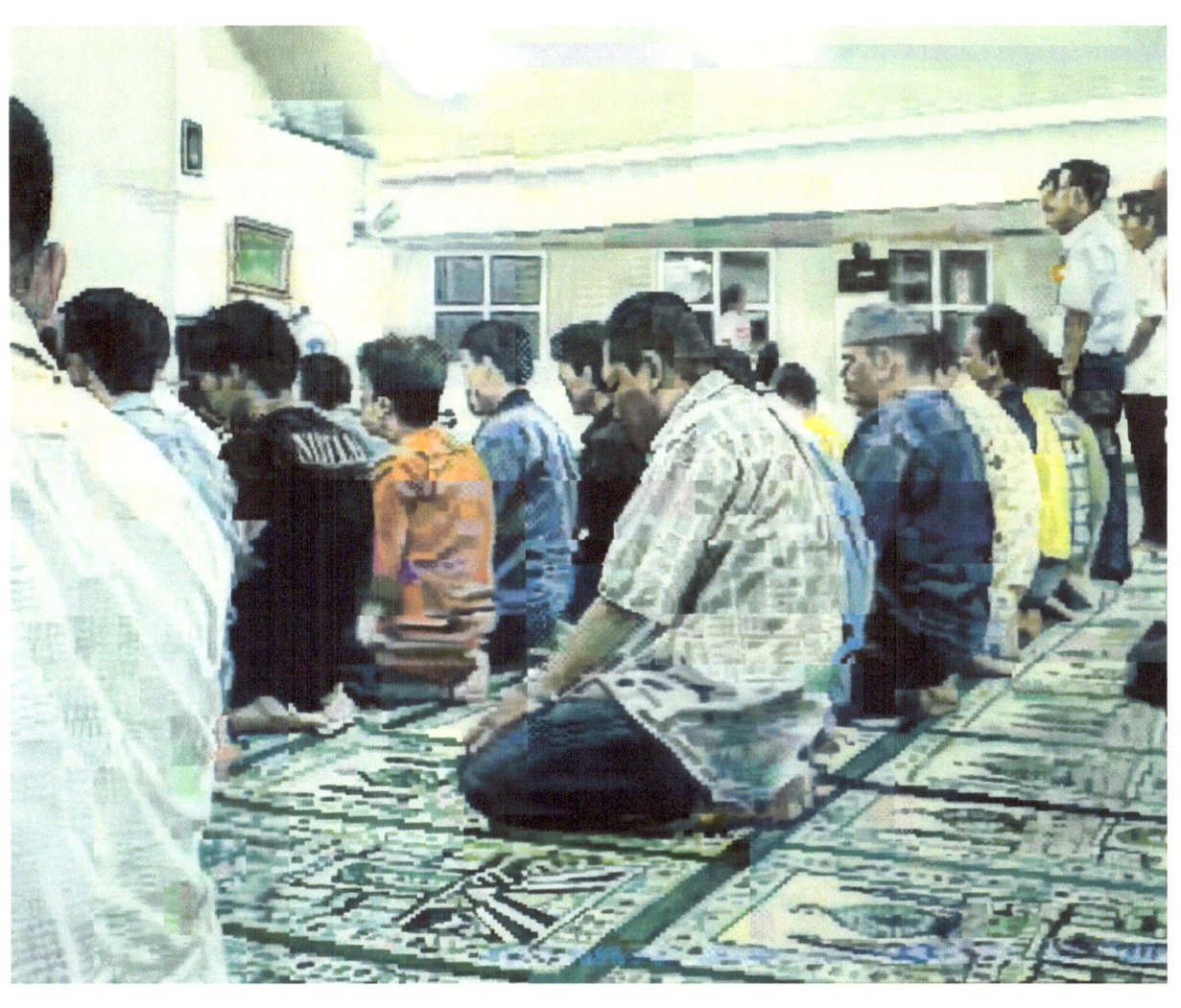

"**Pray** (after chandramarsono)"
(2007) Oil on Canvas 120 x 150 cm

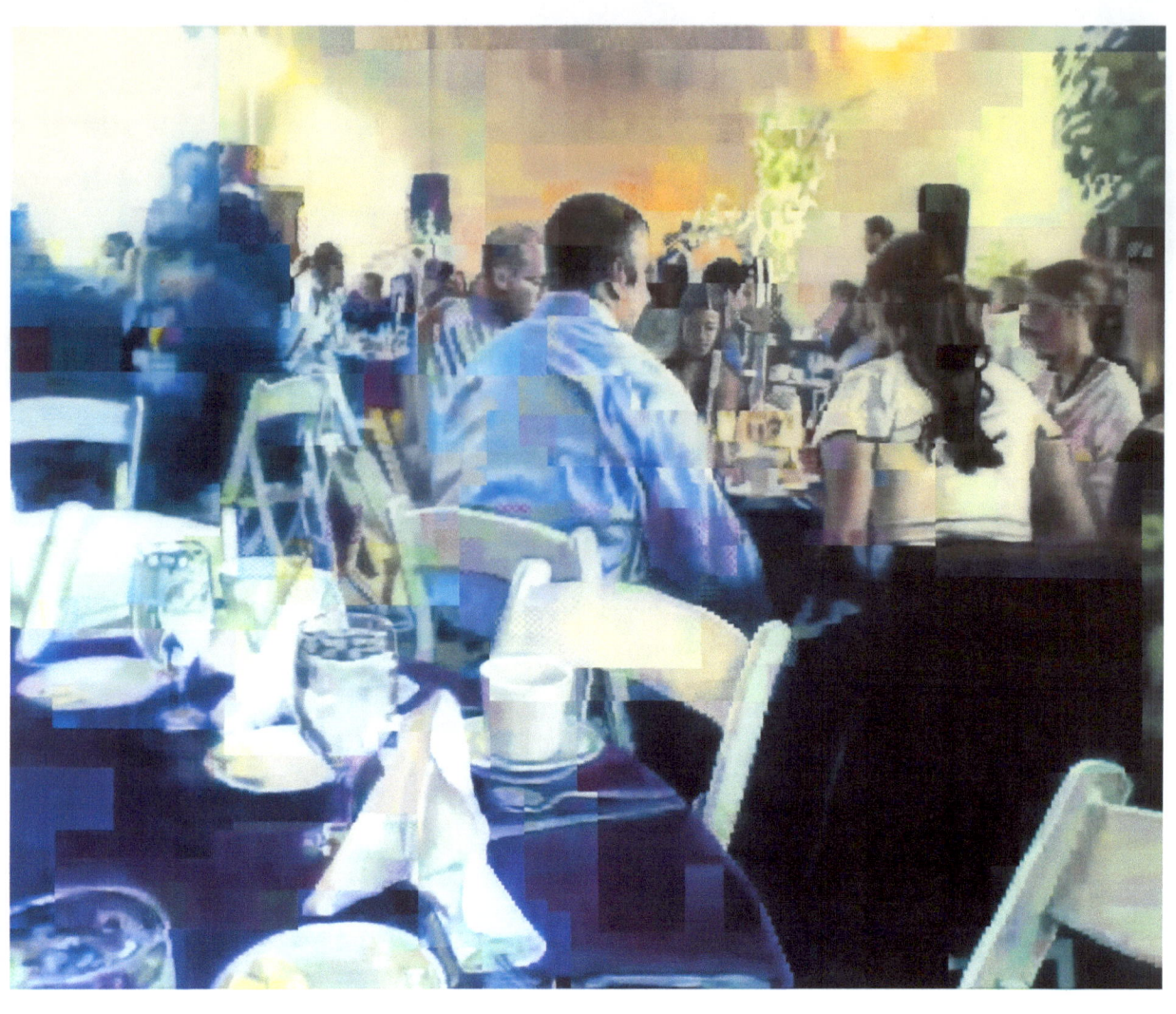

"**Wedding** (after Kaylese)"
(2007) Oil on Canvas 120 x 150 cm

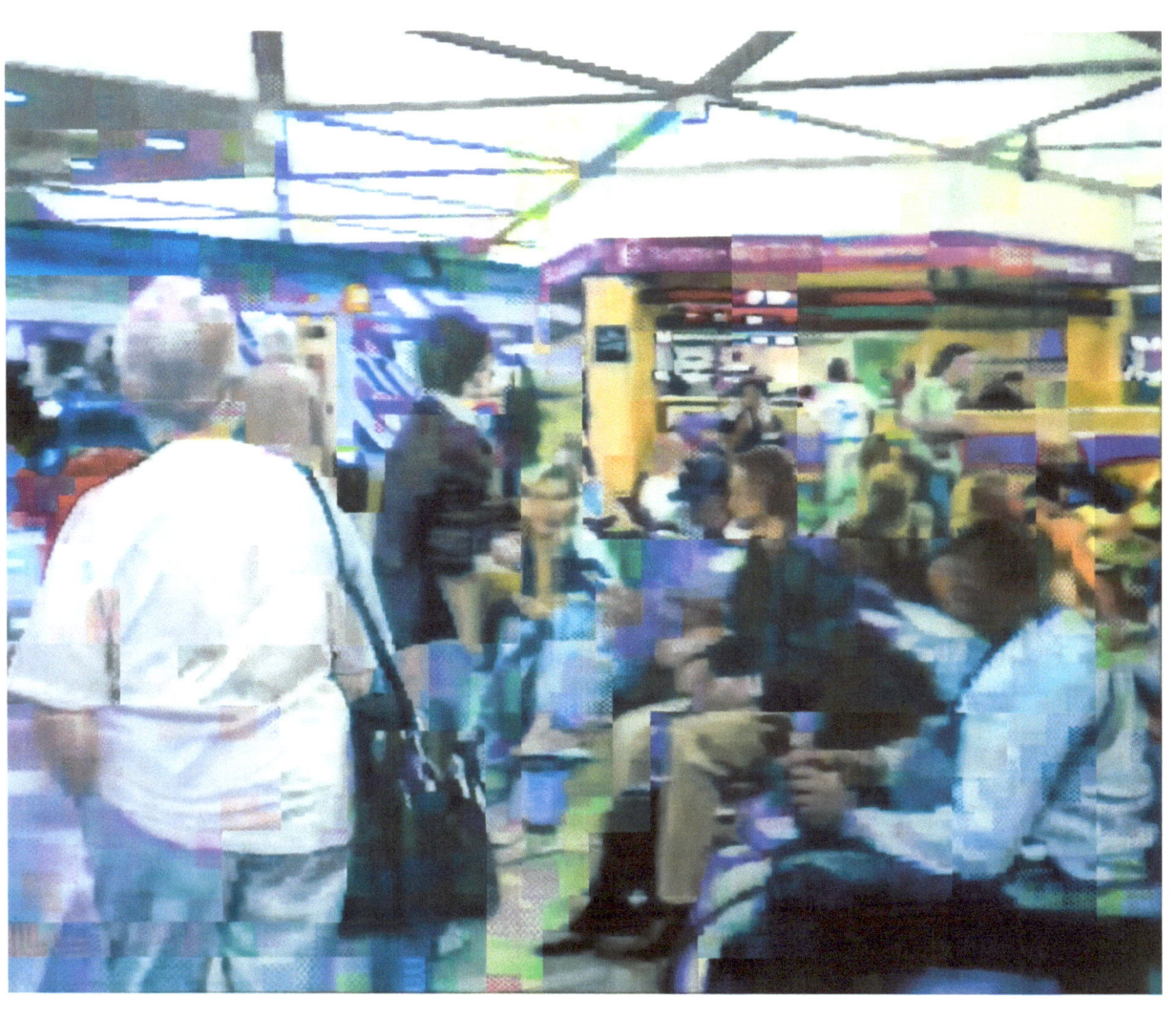

"**Miami** (after Abraxias)"
(2007) Oil on Canvas 120 x 150 cm

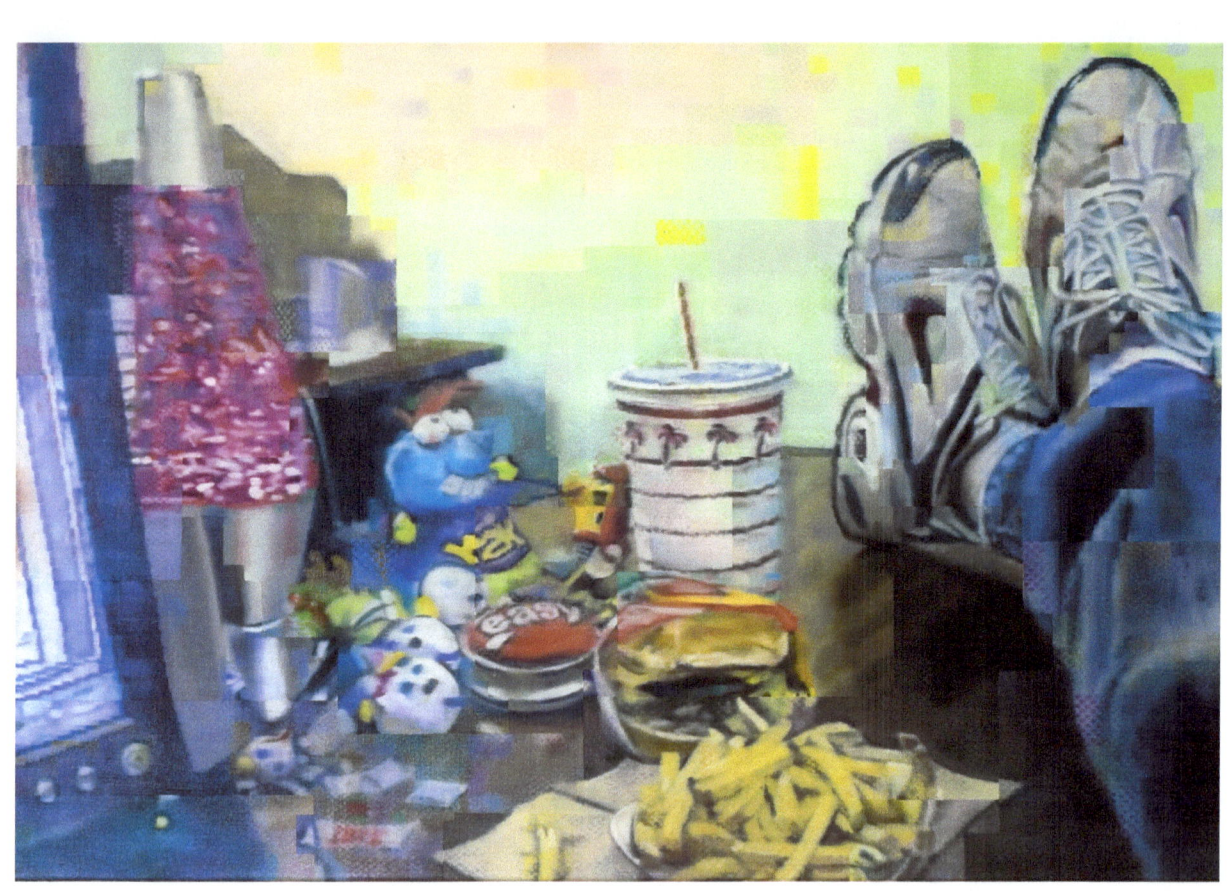

"**Mmmmmmmm** (after Slworking)"
(2007) Oil on canvas 80 x 120 cm

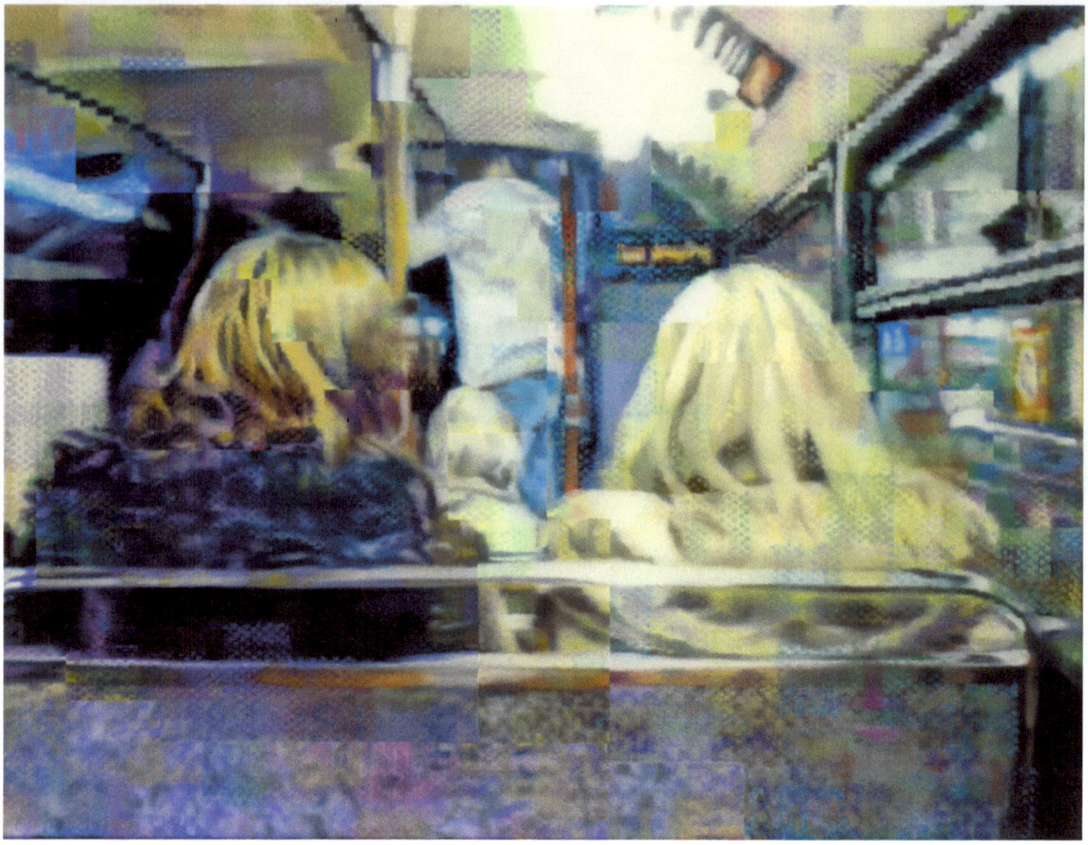

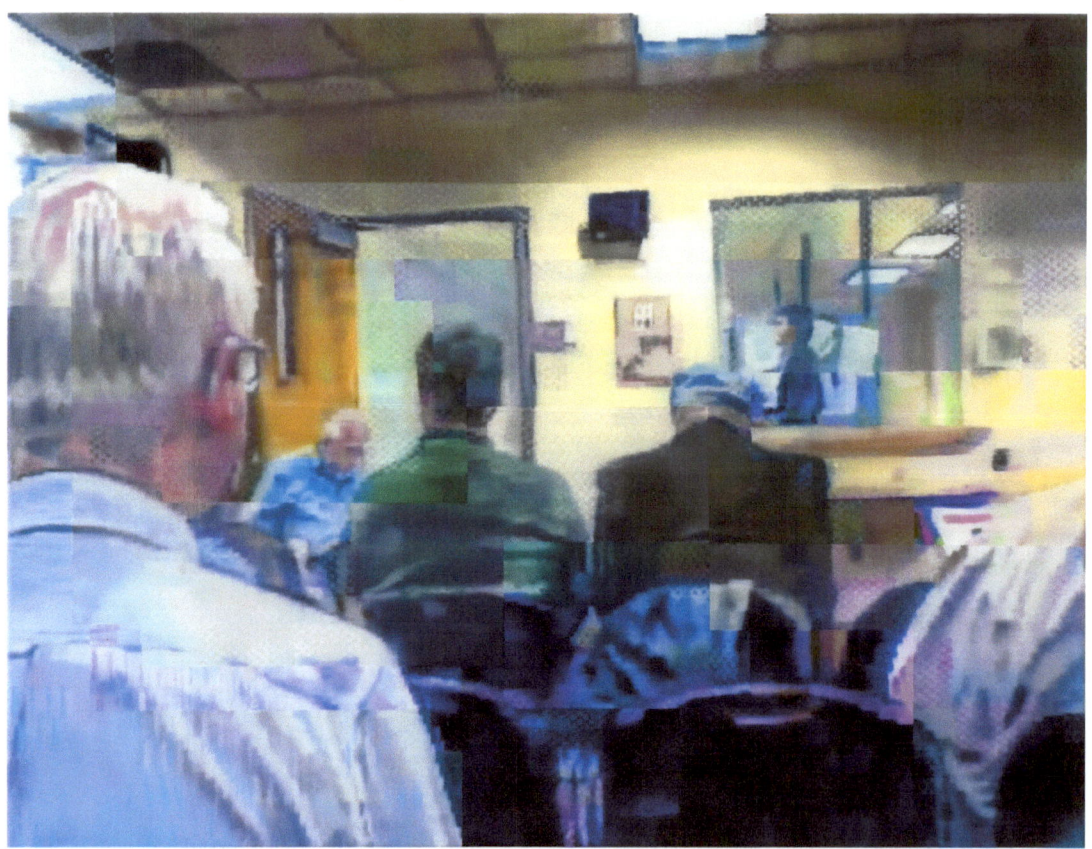

"**Invader** (after agent_vulga)"
(2007) Oil on Canvas 60 x 80 cm

"**Waiting to be called** (after bluebeetle)"
(2007) Oil on Canvas 60 x 80 cm

"First Day New Job (after srage10)"
(2007) Oil on Canvas 60 x 80 cm

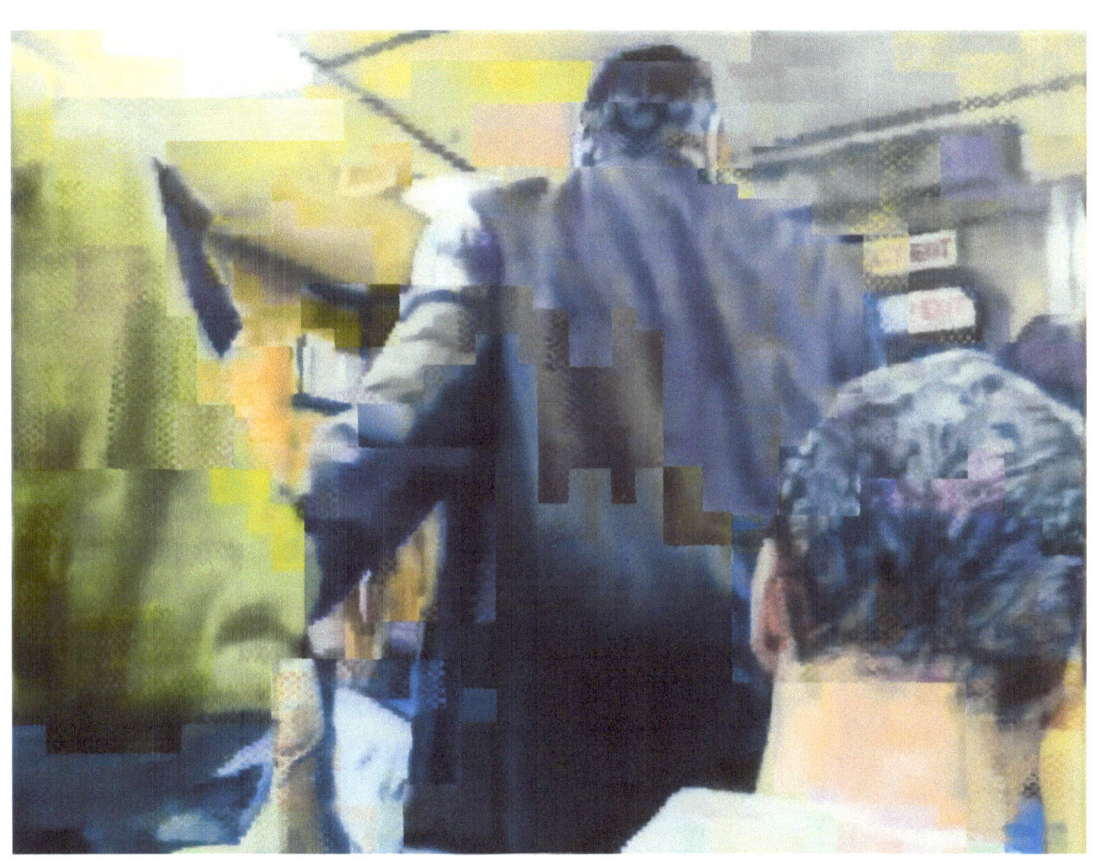

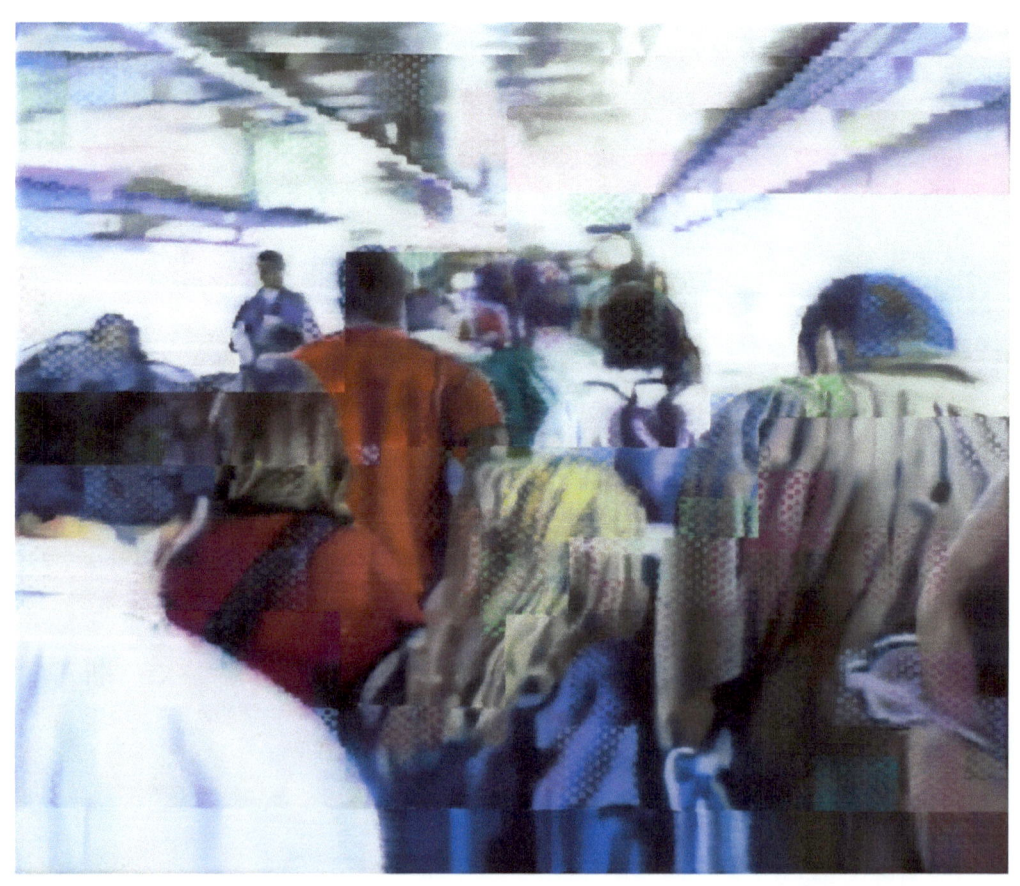

"**Escalator** (after gerrod)"
(2006) Oil on Canvas 50 x 60 cm

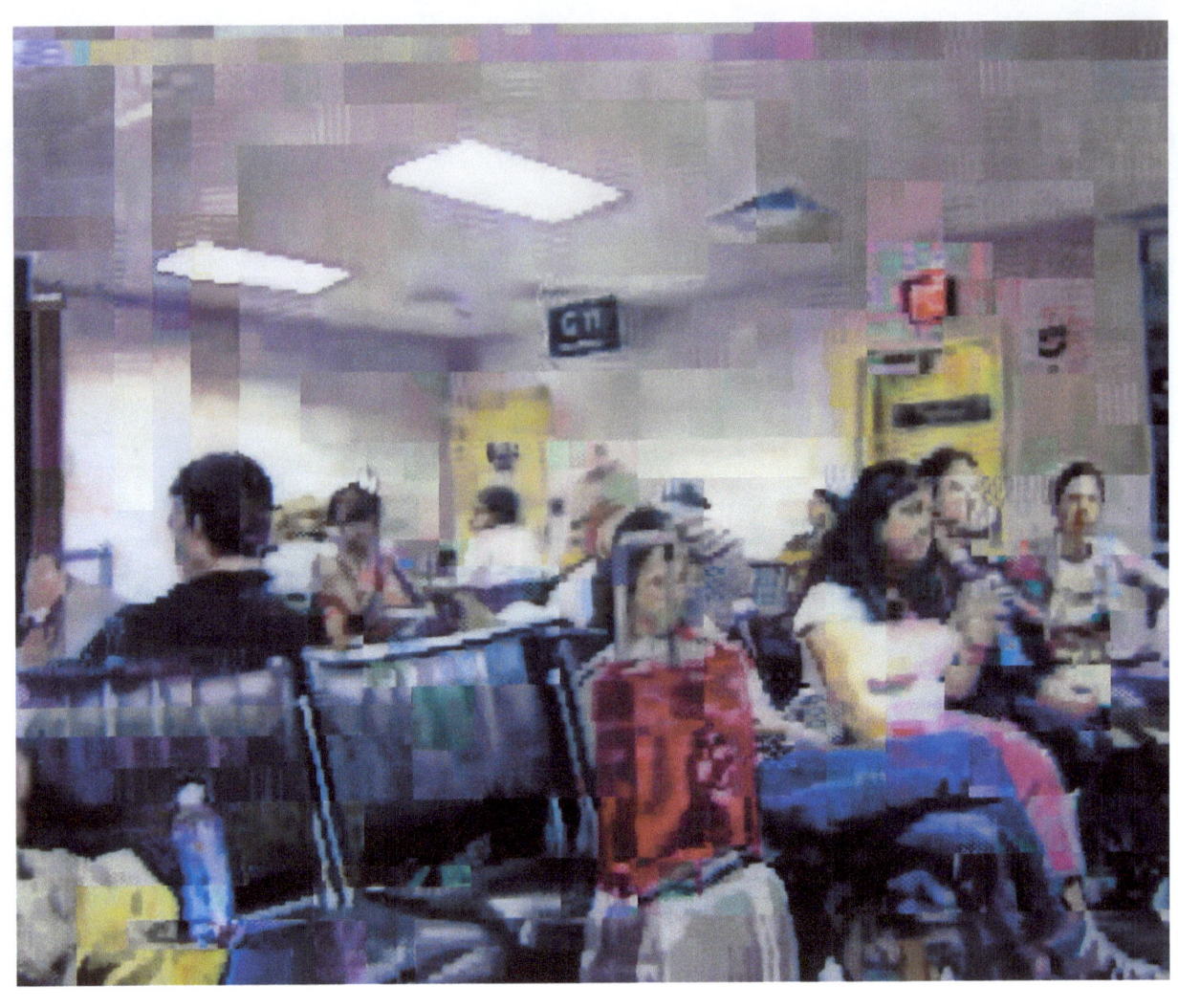

"**To LAX** (after LoKa)"
(2006) Oil on Canvas 120 x 150 cm

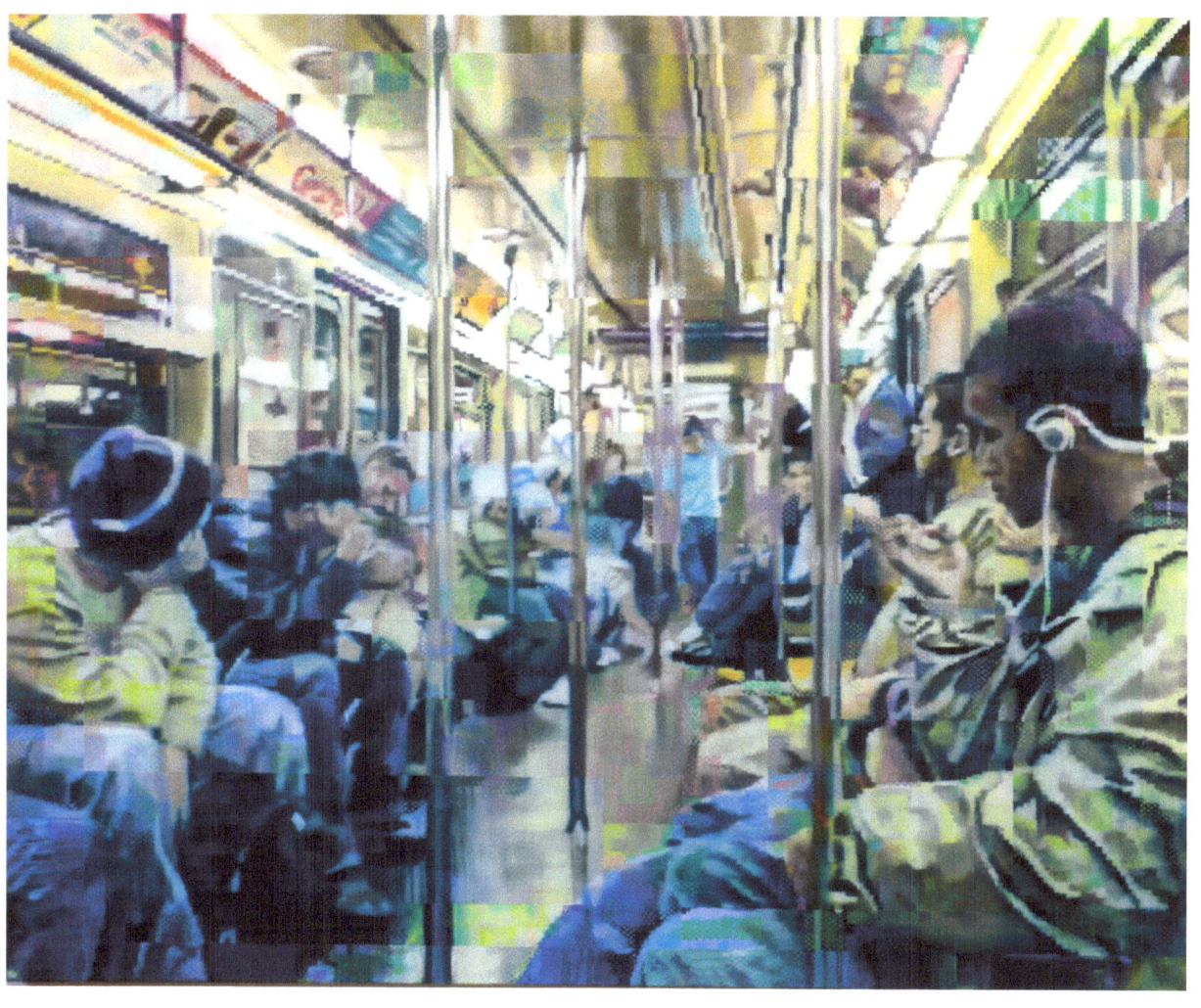

"**On the One** (after JoeBlogs)"
(2006) Oil on Canvas 120 x 150 cm

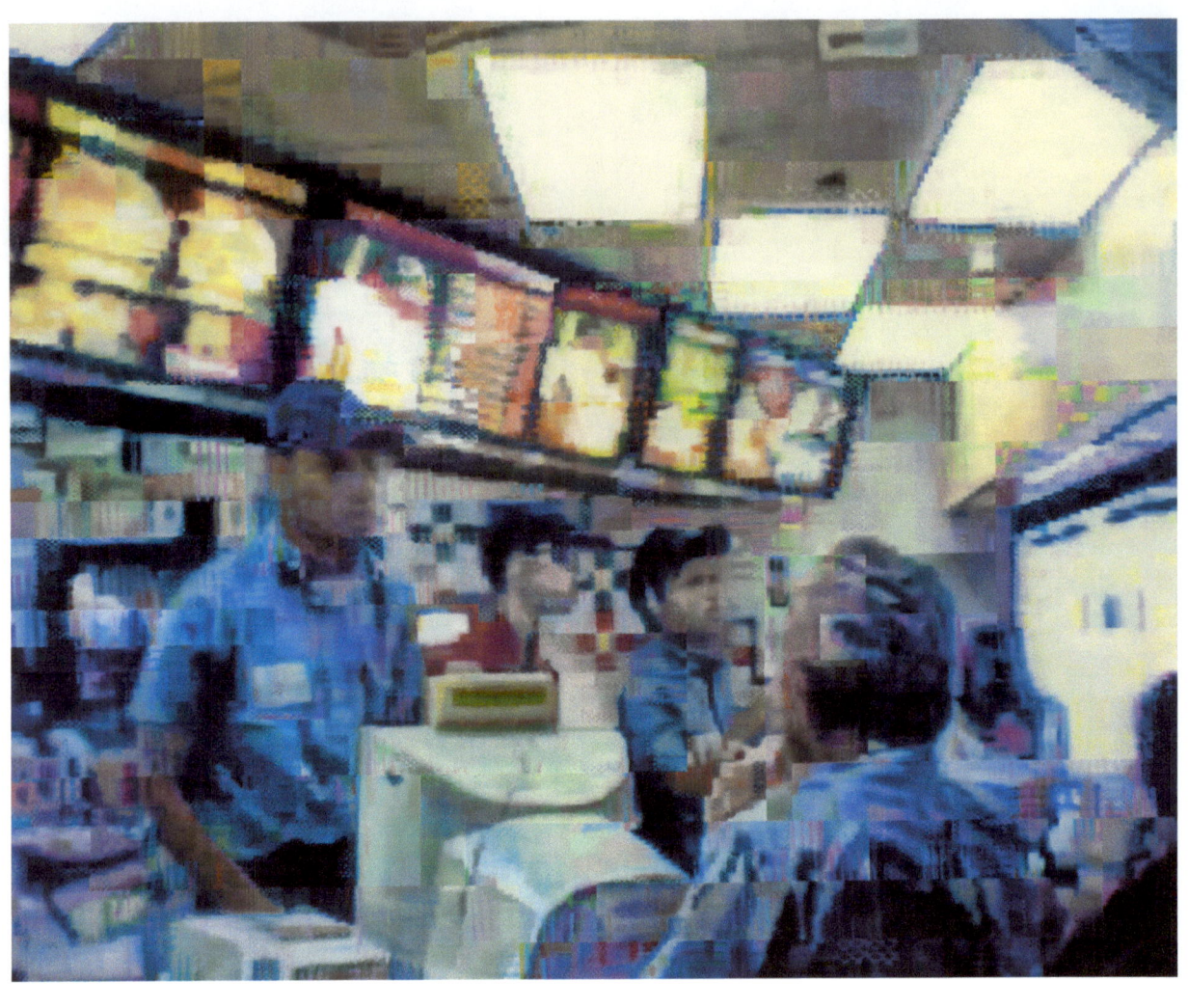

"**The Gain** (after brosjr)"
(2006) Oil on Canvas 120 x 150 cm

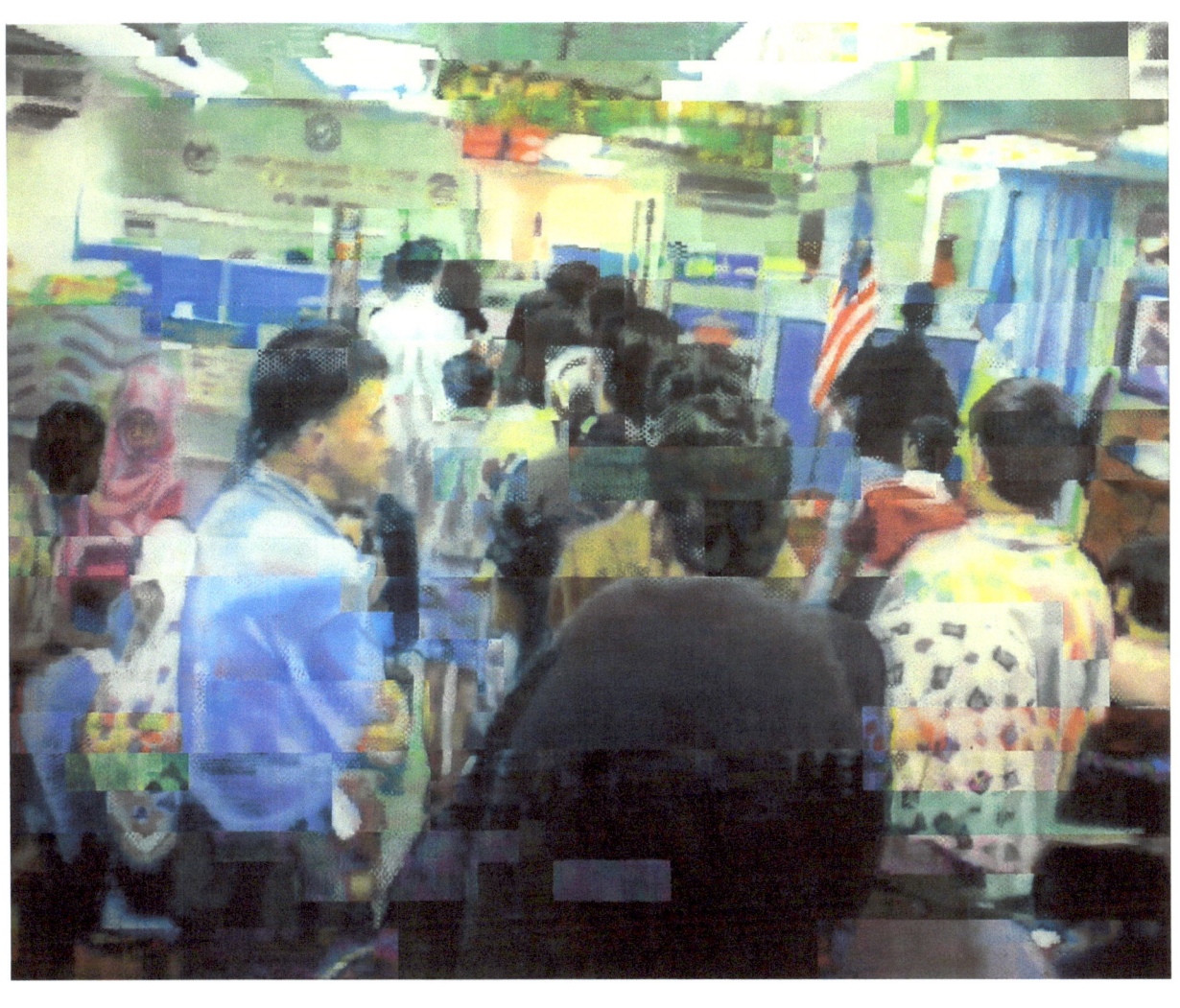

"**Registration** (after Azhari)"
(2006) Oil on Canvas 120 x 150 cm

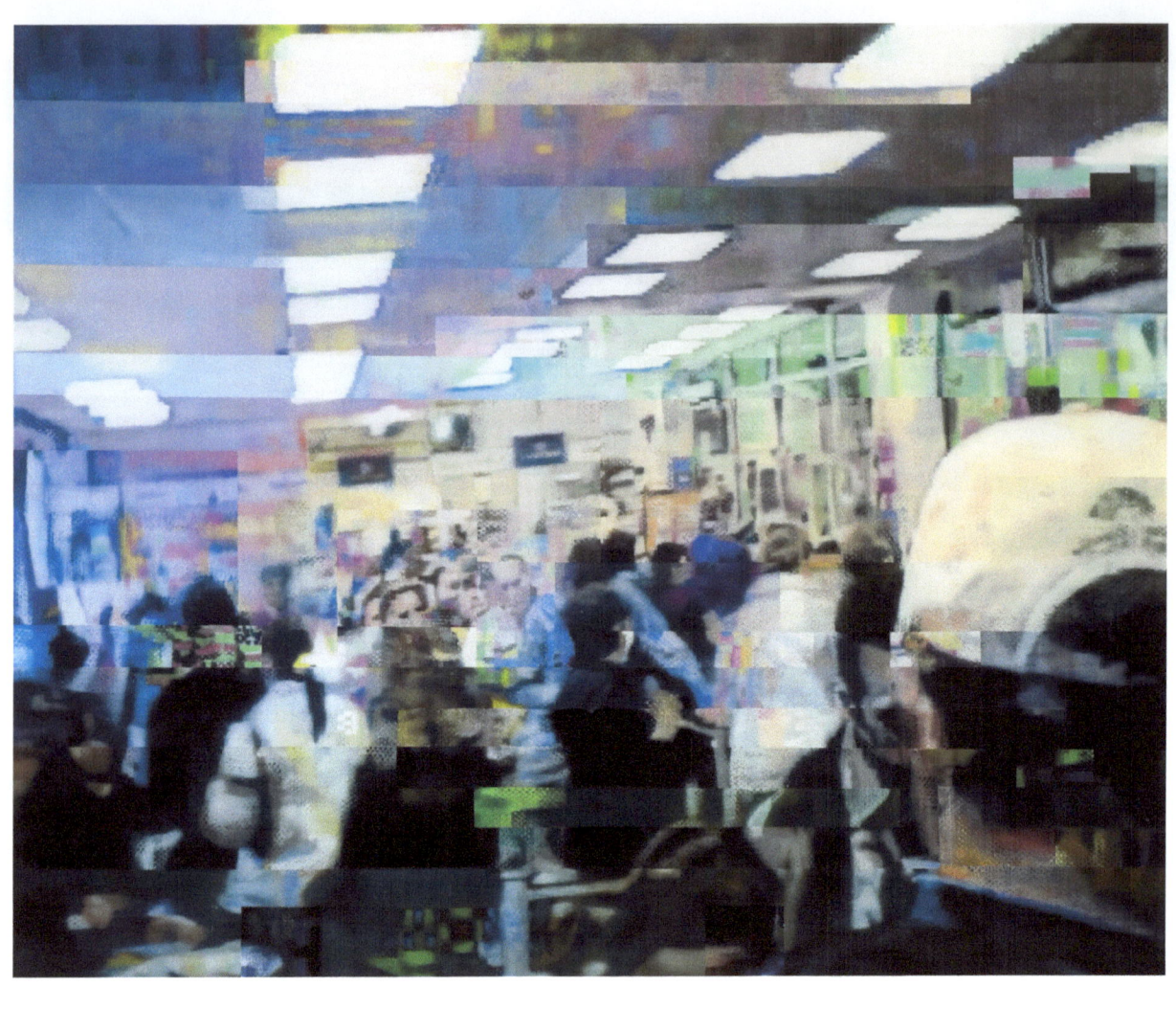

"Stinky Que (after misternavid)"
(2006) Oil on Canvas 120 x 150 cm

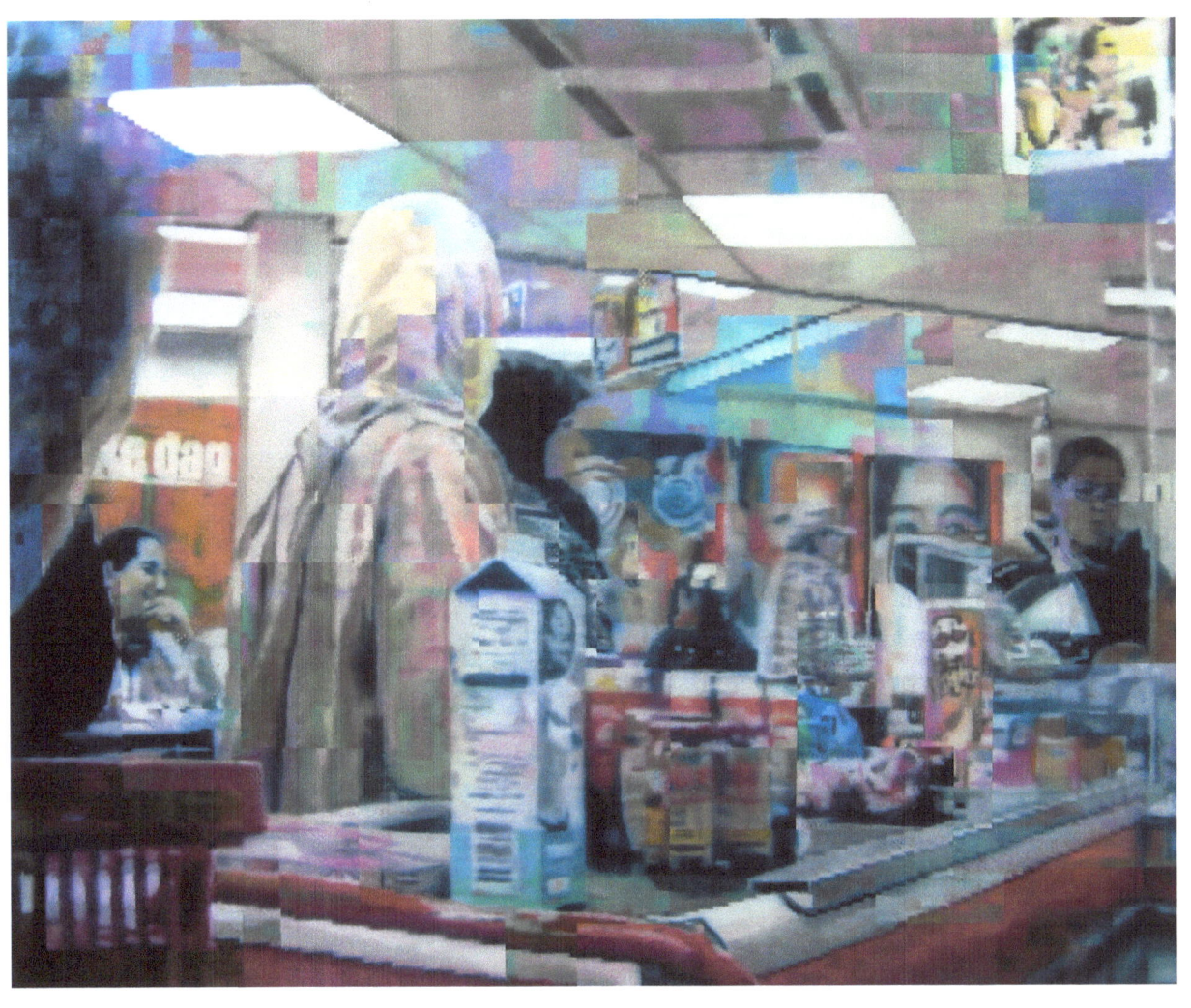

"**Amsterdam** (after Spionnetje)"
(2006) Oil on Canvas 120 x 150 cm

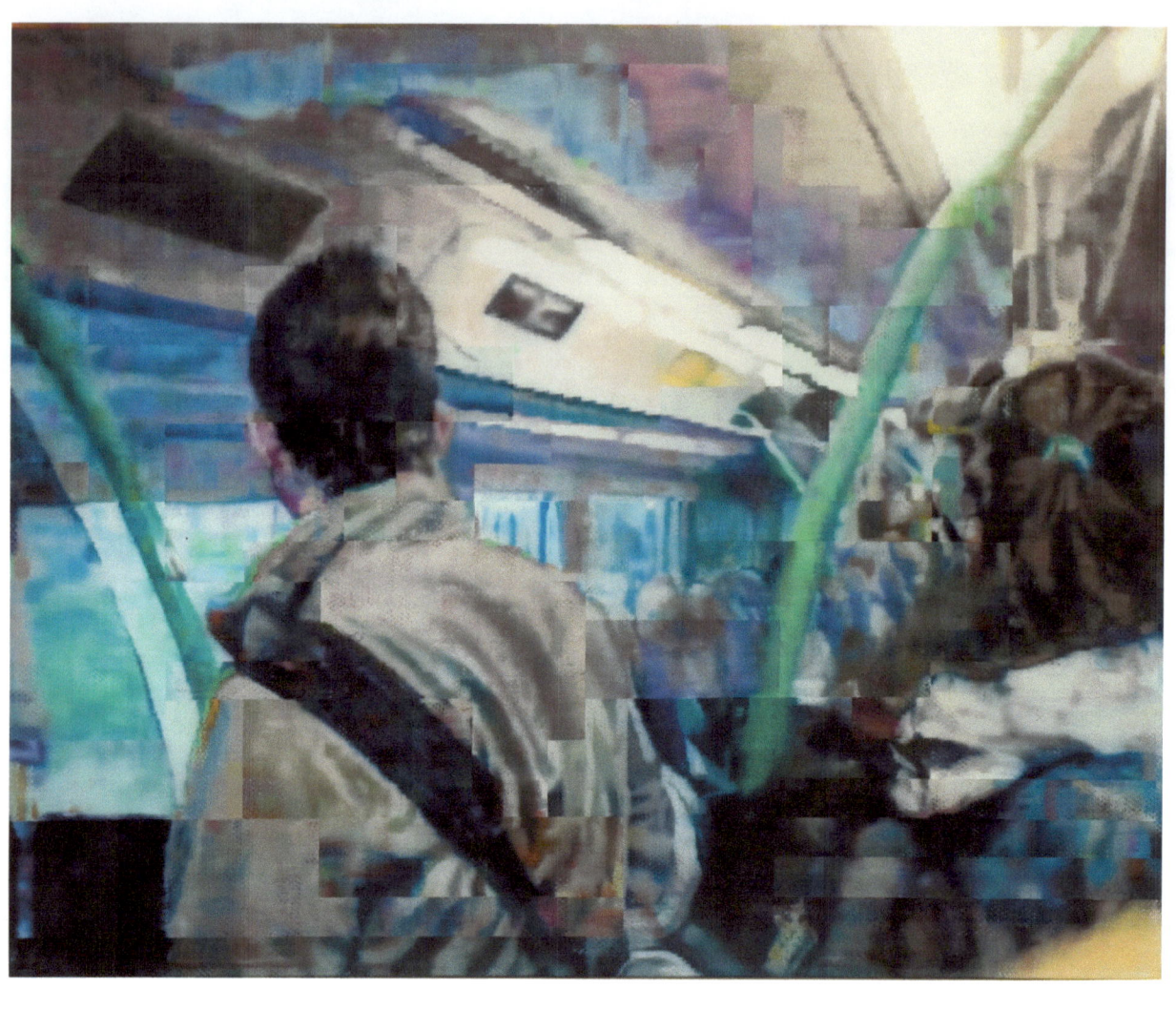

"**Commuter** (after telfon)"
(2006) Oil on Canvas 120 x 150 cm

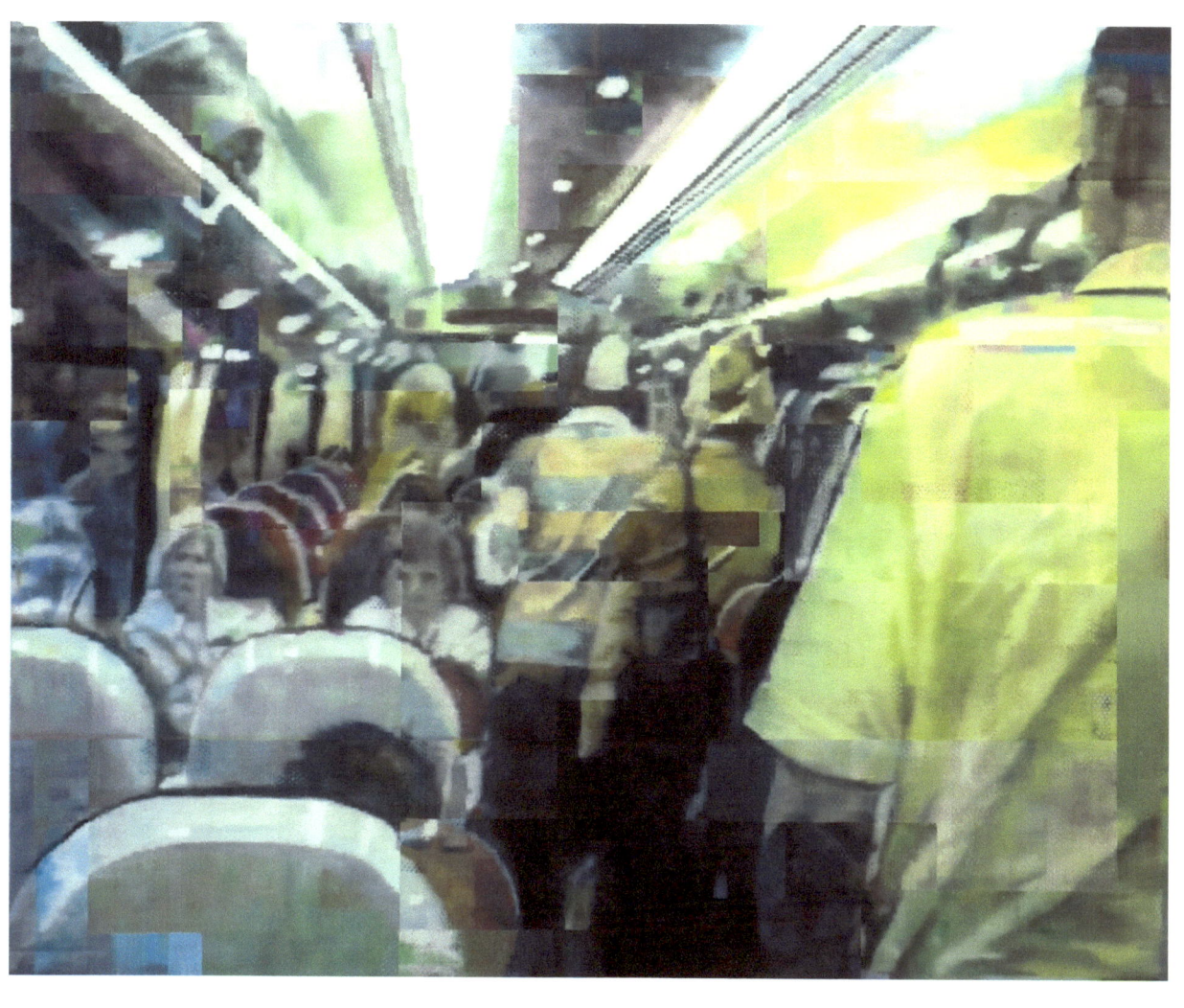

"**The 1604** (after Ruthie)"
(2006) Oil on Canvas 120 x 150 cm

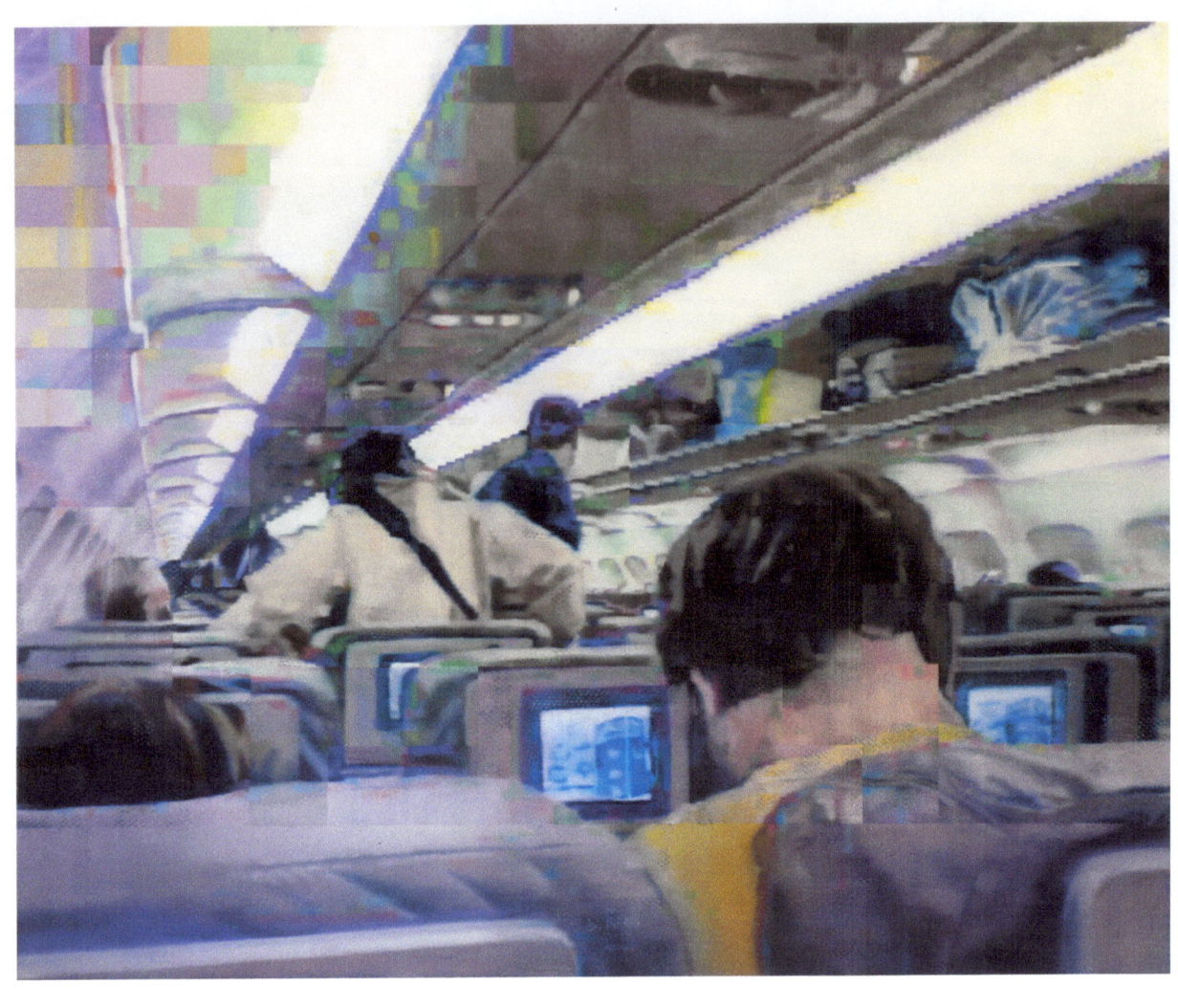

"El Aeroveiculo! (after VenusInFurs)"
(2005) Oil on Canvas 120 x 150 cm

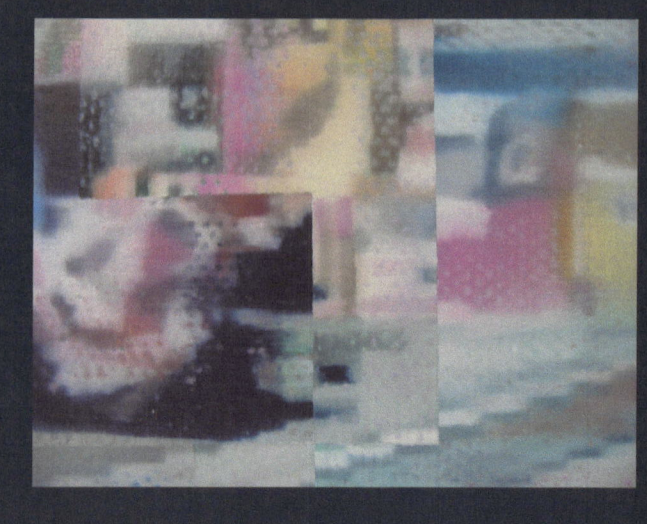

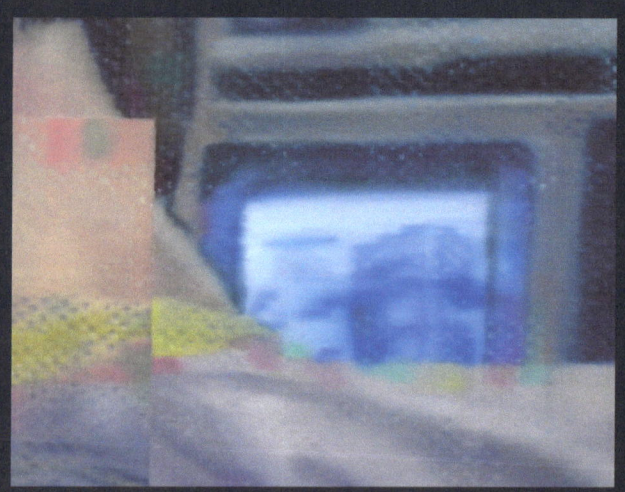

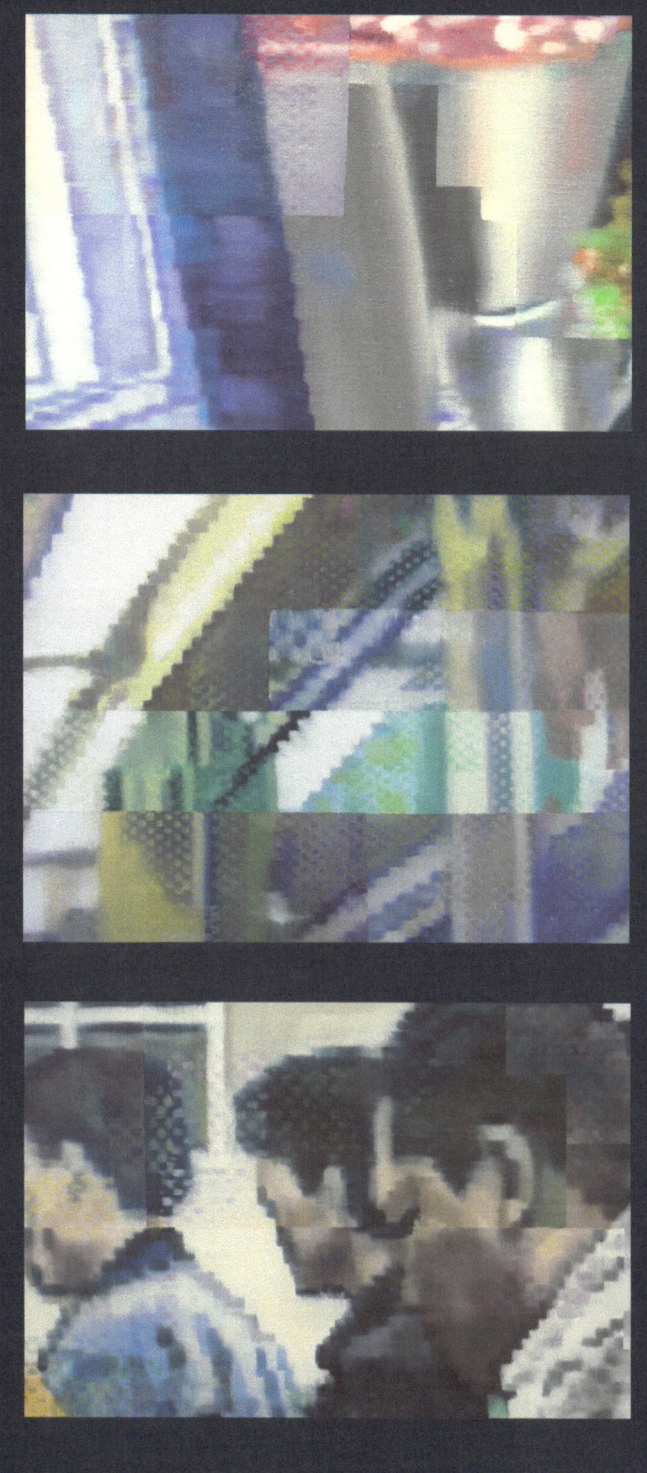

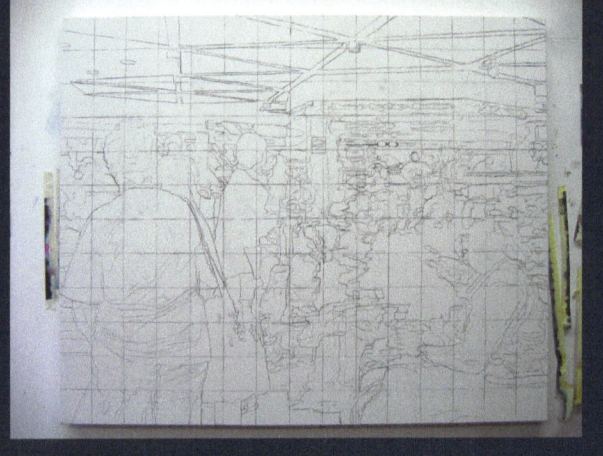
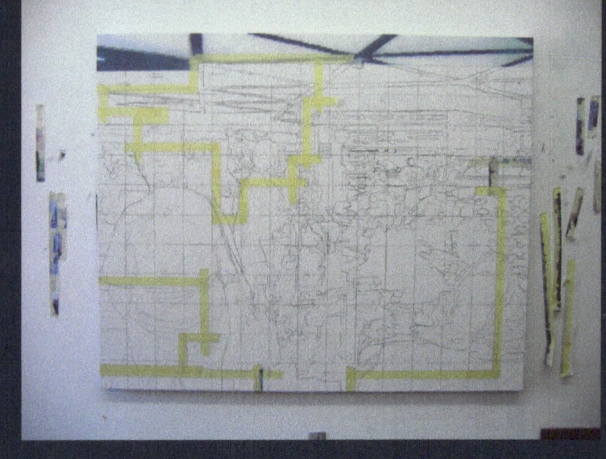
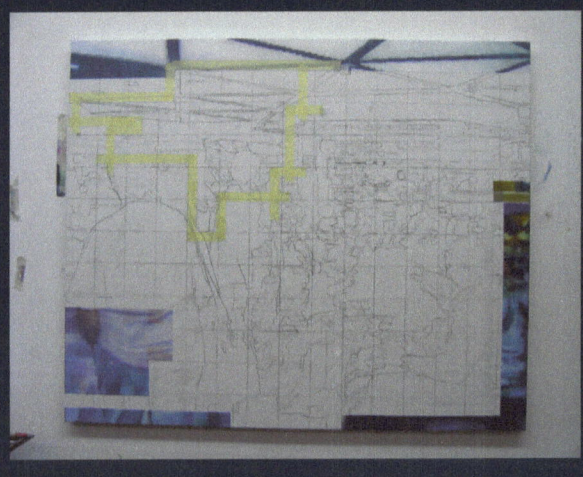
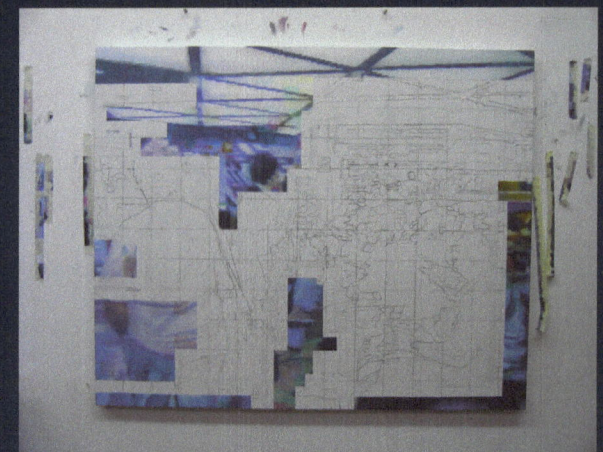
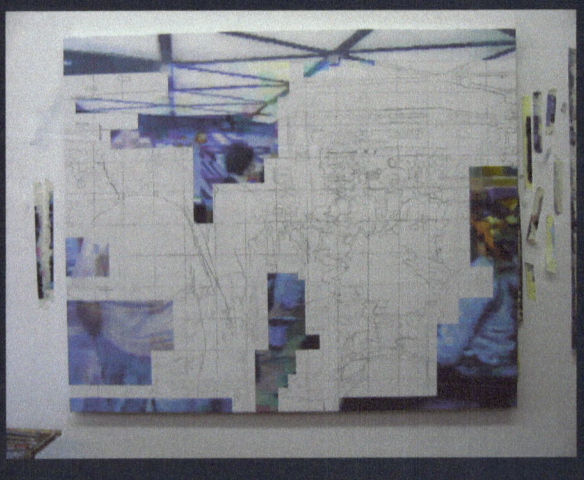
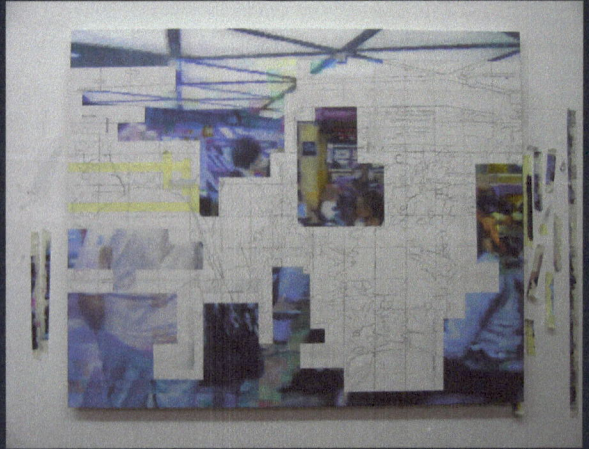

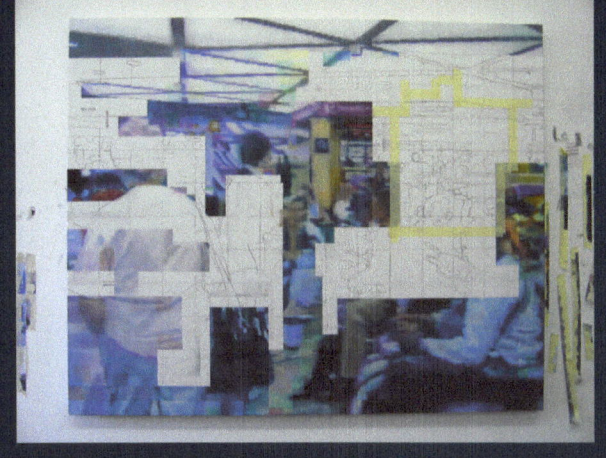
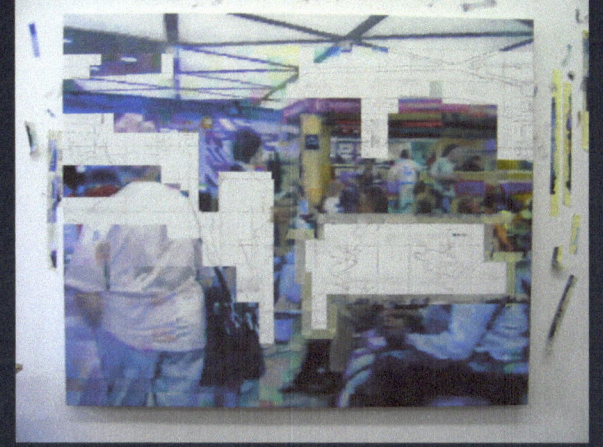
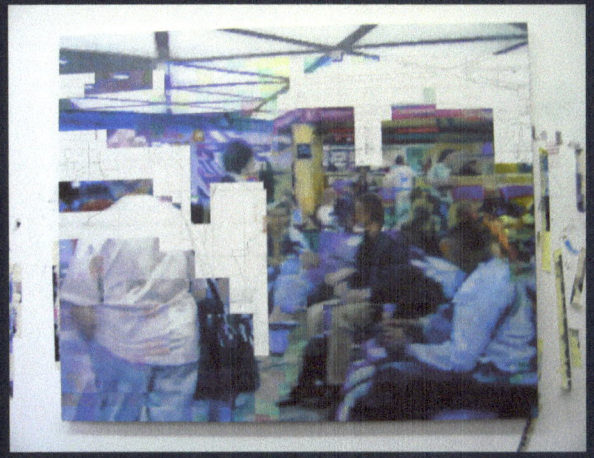
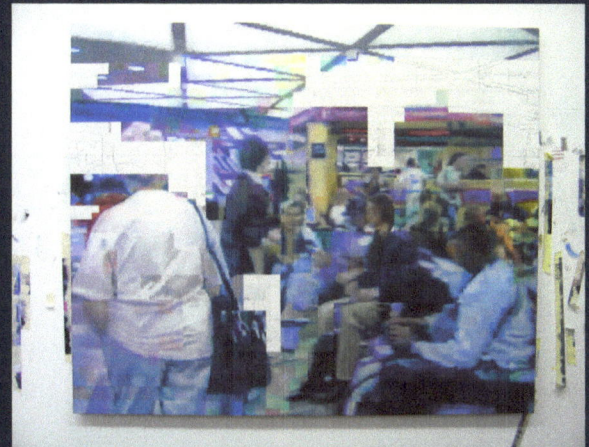
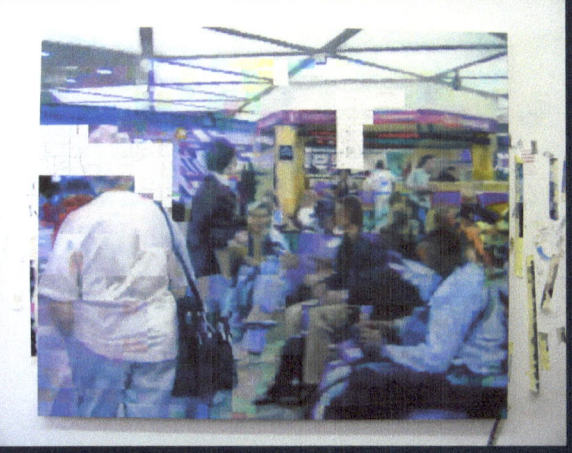
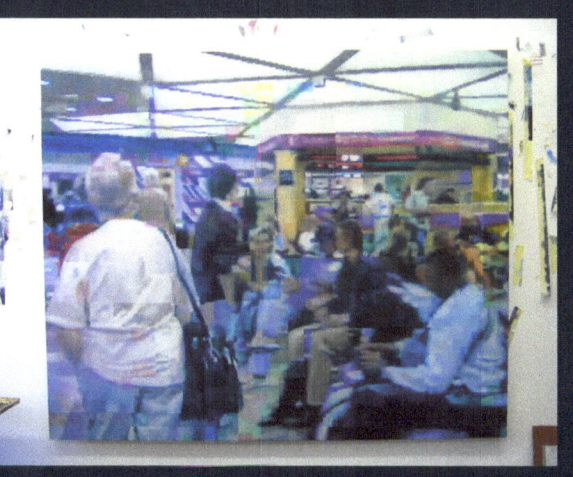

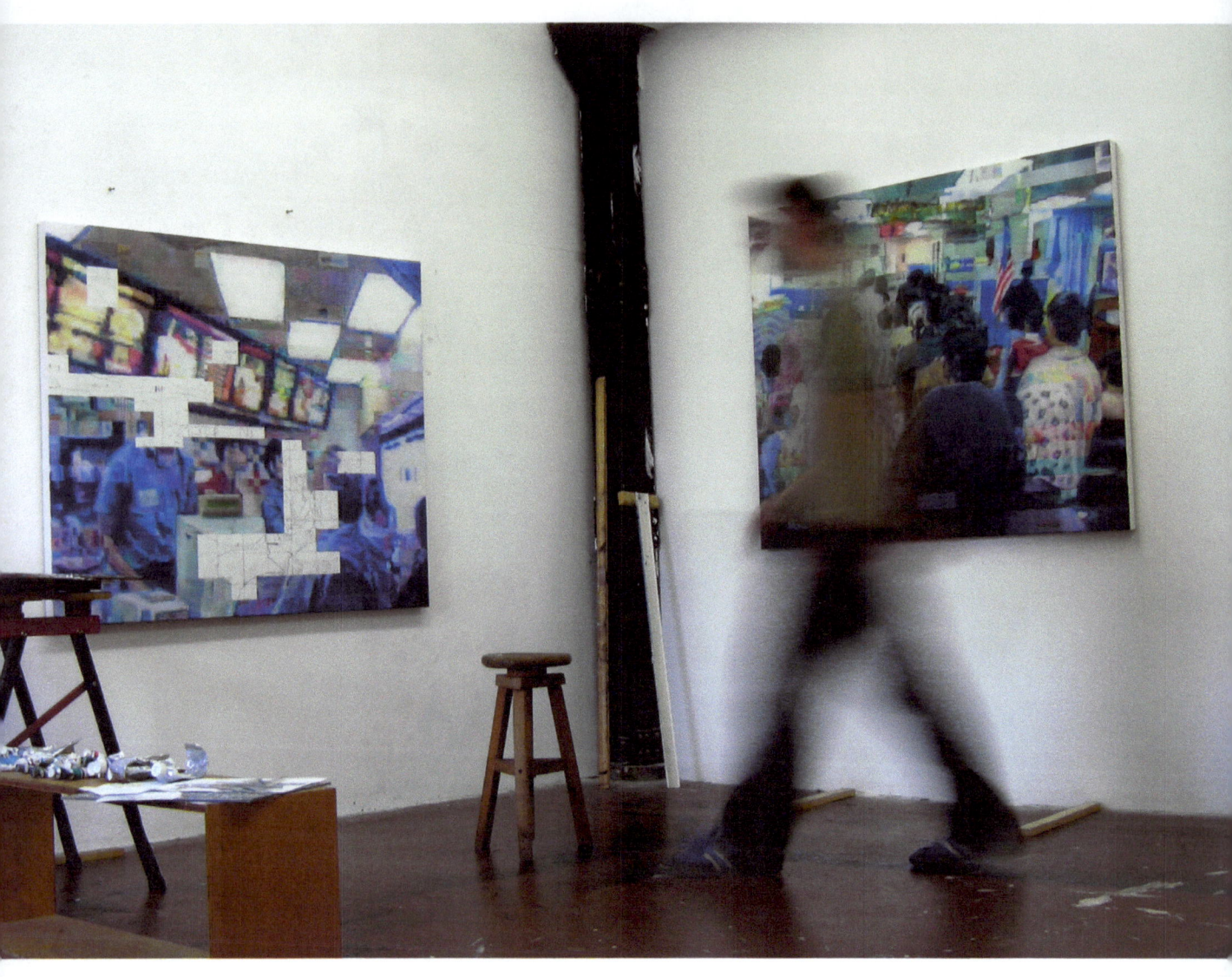

ENDA O'DONOGHUE
born 1973, Limerick, Ireland
currently lives and works in Berlin

email: endaod@endaism.com
website: www.endaism.com

Education:
2000 – Masters of Arts in Interactive Media, University of Limerick, Ireland
1999 – Bachelors Degree in Fine Art, Limerick School of Art & Design

Selected Exhibition Biography:
2007
Solo exhibition – Galerie Hunchentoot, Berlin
4. Berliner Kunstsalon – Berlin – (with Galerie hunchentoot)
HouseSalon 4 – M3 Kunsthalle, Berlin
KIC Nord Art 2007 – Büdelsdorf, Germany
Tease Art Fair – Cologne – (with Weissfaktor Galerie)
Television as Art – Art Channel Galerie 13Sévigné, Paris
Open Source Shorts screening – Darklight Digital, Dublin
Cead in China – Shanghai, Hangzhou and Beijing, China
2006
HouseSalon 3 – M3 Kunsthalle, Berlin
Alternative Art Fair – Fabrikken for Kunst og Design, Copenhagen
boulevART – KunstHerbst Berlin 06, Kurfürstendamm, Berlin
Better than the Real Thing – Four Gallery, Dublin (Curated by Regina Gleeson)
Netfilmmakers at Overgaden – Institute for Contemporary Art, Copenhagen
Open Source Shorts – The Galway Arts Centre, Ireland (Curated by Kevin Flanagan)
2005
Heuriges – M3 Kunsthalle, Berlin
Offside Live II – Hugh Lane Gallery, Dublin
Berliner KunstSalon II – Berliner Pool – Arena Berlin
6x6 for Ireland 2005 – 411 Gallery, Hangzhou, Shanghai and Beijing, China
Solo Exhibition – Kunstsalon Wilde Gans, Berlin
2004
Stafford Film Festival – Beaconside Media Centre – Staffordshire, UK
SALT – film, performing arts event – 291 Gallery, Hackney Rd, London
Wandering Rocks, Revolving Doors – Bank of Ireland, College Green, Dublin
Trampoline (plattform für neue medienkunst) – Prater, Kastanienallee, Berlin
Trace, Traces…- Curator for Group Exhibition – BerlinerKunst Projekt, Berlin
6x6 for Ireland 2004 – 411 Gallery, Hangzhou City, China
Electric Rain – Club One, Phoenix Street, Cork, Ireland
2003
Electronic Image – Stoke Film Theatre, Stoke On Trent, UK
Wexford Artists' Book Exhibition – Wexford Arts Centre, Ireland
Group exhibition – Marzart Galerie, Hamburg, Germany
Launch Option Berlin (Sound Pool Contributor) – BüroFriedrich, Berlin
Moviemiento – Project at the u-site-fusion-festival – Flugplatz Lärz, Germany

2002
Darklight Film Digital Festival 4 – Thomas Street, Dublin
EV+A 2002 – St. John the Baptist Church, Limerick, Ireland
Temporary Public Installation (with Edel McWeeney) – University of Limerick, Ireland
Hope and Homes – Dooradoyle Library, Limerick, Ireland
2001
Eject IV (Real Art Project Video Show) – Dolan's Warehouse, Limerick, Ireland
Ouch!electro Collaboration Group – Limerick Printmaker's, Robert St, Limerick, Ireland
2000
Immediate Release – University of Limerick, Ireland
1999
Ado Enough Done (Solo Exhibition) – Catherine St., Limerick, , Ireland
Eject II (Real Art Project Video Show) – Flannery's, Catherine St., Limerick, Ireland
1998
Wexford Artists' Book Exhibition – Wexford Arts Festival, Ireland
HUNT – Hunt Museum, Limerick, Ireland
Demanding the Impossible – Temple Bar Gallery, Dublin
The City (Temporary Public Art Event) – Cruises Street, Limerick, Ireland
Photography Exhibition – City gallery at City Hall, Limerick, Ireland
1997
Atelier photographique – Galerie de l'école des Beaux-Arts, Quimper, France

Additional Information:
2005 - Present
Member of the Berliner Pool, artist archive – www.berlinerpool.de
2004
Invited participant for Joyce in Art, discussion – Royal Hibernian Gallery, Dublin
Invited guest lecturer to Institute of Technology Tralee, Ireland
2002
Visiting lecturer to the Limerick School of Art and Design
2000 - 2002
Interactive Media Lecturer & Course Coordinator – Interaction Design Centre, University of Limerick, Ireland
Exhibition Coordinator DAWN '01 & '02 (Digital Arts Week Now) University of Limerick
2000
Multimedia Tutor – Limerick School of Art and Design
Invited guest speaker to MIT Media Lab Europe Bellevue, Dublin 8, Ireland
1998 - 2001
Member of the artists-run organisation "The Real Art Project" based in Limerick, Ireland

Brief Bibliography:

"Postcards from the Digital-Atomic Border" by R. T. Jim Eales and Dharani Perera, research paper, IADIS, Lisbon, Portugal, 2007

"Better than the real thing?" by Paul O'Brien, CIRCA, Issue 117, Ireland, Autumn 2006, pp. 94-96

"Following the Lead" by Billy Leahy, Village Magazine, Dublin, Ireland, Issue 89, June 2006, p 55

"Hangzhou: 6x6 for Ireland at 411 Gallery" by Arvo Bruene, CIRCA, Issue 109, Ireland, Autumn 2004, pp.82-83

"Wandering Rocks, Revolving Doors" by Susan Saskash, The Visual Artists' News Sheet, Sculptors' Society of Ireland (SSI), Issue Five, 2004

"Wandering Rocks, Revolving Doors" (James Joyce et l'art public) by P-Y Desaive, Flux News, Liège, Belgium, July 2004

"Kunst ist Lüge", (Spuren: Zu einer Ausstellung im Berliner Kunst-Projekt) by Jürgen Schneider, junge welt, Berlin, Germany, 01.04.2004

Catalogues:

4. Berliner Kunstsalon, Catalogue, Kunstverein Rhein Ruhr e.V. Berlin, Germany, 2007

"Céad in China", Catalogue, 411 Galleries, China, 2007

NordArt 07, Kunst in der Carlshütte GmbH, Büdelsdorf, Germany, 2007

"Tease issue #1", Tease Art Fair Catalogue, Kunstverein Rhein Ruhr e.V. Cologne, Germany, 2007

KunstHerbst Berlin 06 Programmheft, Sept. 2006

"6x6 for Ireland, Showcase 2005" Catalogue, 411 Galleries, China, 2005

"EV+A 2002: heroes + holies" Catalogue, Edited by Paul M O'Reilly, Gandon Editions, Ireland, 2002

Second edition

Acknowledgments:
Hannes Uhlemann, Brian Coates, Jürgen Schneider
Connie Wagner and the staff of OktoberDruck.
Helen Smith and Lisa McElligott for design and layout assistance
and advice.
Nicholas Grindell, Anne-Sophie Fraysse, Regina Gleeson,
Sibylle Jazra, Ilona Ottenbreit, Jim Eales, Amanda Dunsmore,
Eoghan McTigue, MJ Whelan...

for the permission to use their images: Abraxias, agent_vulga,
Azhari, brosjr, gerrod, JoeBlogs, LoKa, misternavid, Ruthie,
Spionnetje, telfon, VenusInFurs, Slworking, chandramarsono,
srage10, bluebeetle, Kaylese, prestonm, sydusa, Hopper,
justinsomnia

and finally
Noah, Émile
and Raphaëlle

Produced in cooperation with

hunchentoot

Galerie für zeitgenössische
Positionen

Choriner Straße 8, 10119 Berlin
www.galerie-hunchentoot.de

and with the support of Culture Ireland

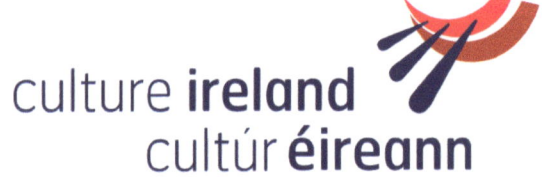

promoting the arts abroad
cur chun cinn na n-ealaíon thar lear

www.ingramcontent.com/pod-product-compliance
Lightning Source LLC
Chambersburg PA
CBHW050905180526
45159CB00007B/2795